WE

Are

Church

John Chuchman

This book was printed in
The United States of America by Booksurge.com

Additional copies of this book
and copies of the author's other titles

"Springtime in Autumn,"
"Pebbles of Wisdom,"
"Quest,"
"Sunset Awakening," and
"Journeying Through Life"
"I Love My Church, BUT OH MY GOD!"

may be ordered from Amazon.com
or from the author at

poetman@torchlake.com
www.torchlake.com/poetman

Introduction

The reaction to my last book

"I Love My Church,
BUT OH MY GOD!"

was so encouraging

that I decided to share more
of my writings

related to Church.

Though I have been anxious to move away
from writing about the issues facing

Institutional Church

and return to more spiritual
and more positive topics,

the continued

non-transparency, non-accountability

of Church Hierarchy

compels me to speak out.

Love,

John Chuchman

Aspects, Essence, Distinctions of My Faith

I believe that
God Sanctifies All Aspects of Our Existence on Earth.

Salvation is not to be found or holiness achieved
by scorning reality
or trying to escape all that is human,
but by
Living Life Fully.

By embracing all that is human
(the good and the bad)
all things are transformed by Grace
and become a means to Redemption.

On the path of Spiritual Growth
we must often descend
in order to ascend.

Often, the way up is down.

The Path is a daily struggle,
a long road
of engaging the world
with ups and downs,
fits and starts.

I believe that God,
Is not only transcendent,
but also
Immanent in the world.

All things that exist,
do so because God created them,
God loves them,
and God sustains them,
and thus
all things have the ability to
communicate the Power and Goodness of God.

God is intimately with us
in the Eucharist,
and in all circumstances,
and at all times.

The Sacred is Continuous with the secular.

All created things emanate from God
and reveal God.
All of Creation is essentially Good.

God dwells with us on earth,
animating and transforming everything
making all of Creation
Sacramental.

I believe that
Humans, as created beings,
are designed for a Noble End.
Human Life is precious.

Our Life Journey is fraught with meaning.

With Free Will to accept or reject
The Noble Challenge to a High and Dignified Calling,
Human Life is intensely dramatic.

Our struggles are significant.

My Faith is Optimistic.

Where there is Life, there is Hope.

No matter how tragic are life's events,
my Faith rejects despair.

I am always hopeful.

My Faith does not take me out of the world,
but ever deeper into it.

My Faith
Is steeped in Mystery
and an intense Delight in Creation.

My Faith
is lofty while sensual,
and
Heaven-directed while earthbound.

Human Life on earth is Mystery,
an intersection of the Natural and Supernatural.

Bankrupt?

One more diocese has entered into bankruptcy, because the diocese, not willingly, is being forced to pay just compensation

to many survivors of sexual abuse.

A tragedy?

What's so desperately sad about that?

The Church is supposed to be poor, isn't it?

Imagine the community of disciples of Jesus having to declare bankruptcy?

What would they be giving up?

They weren't rich.

Jesus wasn't rich.

He gave up possessions.

He lived poorly.

For a few hundred years, the church had no property, had no buildings.

There was a community of disciples following the way of Jesus.

Instead of deploring the fact

that a diocese goes bankrupt,

every diocese ought to be void of possessions.

We ought to be a church of the poor.

We're not.

Institutional Church has extraordinary wealth.

Far from being a church of the poor,

especially here in our country,

the church is moving away from the poor.

Some people stay

and continue to proclaim God's Word,

but often it's not Institutional Catholic church.

That's very sad, very sad

that our Church is really not willing to do

what Jesus asks of us.

"Go sell everything.

Give it all up and then enter into the Reign of God,

enter into the work of transforming God's world into

the Reign of God."

In an encyclical letter written back in 1967,

Pope Paul VI called upon all of us

to look carefully at what we have

and how much we have.

He asked the question, quoting St. John's first letter,

"How does the love of God abide in any person

who has the goods of this world

and closes his or her heart to someone in need?"

The love of God does not abide in such a person.

Paul VI goes on to tell us,

teaching out of the tradition of the church

and out of the Scriptures that,

"No one has the right to keep for your own use

what is beyond your need

when others lack the barest necessities."

We don't have a right to keep for our use

what is beyond our need

when others lack the barest necessities.

In a city where
one out of five children is living in poverty,
is there anyone of us who's here today that could
say,
"I don't have something in excess
that I could share with the poor?"
Every one of us has to face up to this.

"Go and sell what you have,
give it all up, give it to the poor
and then come and follow me."
And this is the other part that's so difficult –

to really follow Jesus,

especially in following that way of love.

Are we giving up any of our weapons?

No.

Are we building new weapons?

Yes.

Are we determined to use them?

Yes.

Is that following the way of Jesus?

Of course it's not!

Look at the Amish community –

a community that is living poorly;

they don't have huge churches and so on.

They're following Jesus.

And, when they suffered that terrible tragedy,

do they want to get revenge?

Do they try to use violence to get even?

No.

When the killer is buried,

there are about 75 people there

over half of them are from the Amish community,
following the way of love.

It's possible, but it's certainly a challenge, isn't it?

Think of Jesus looking upon any one of us with love,

tremendous love, and saying,

"Go sell what you have, give it away, come follow
me."

And instead of being like the man in the Gospel

going away sad,

beg God to help us

because it's only possible with God.

Beg God to help us,

to begin to rid ourselves of our excess wealth

and truly to follow Jesus

and his way of love.

Being Catholic

I grew up thinking that being Catholic meant

Going to Mass every Sunday,
Confessing at least once a year—or more,
Not eating meat on Fridays,
Fasting during Lent,
Praying the Rosary,
Making Novenas,
Believing in the Authority of the Pope, and
The Seven Sacraments.

I identified my Faith with
the external observances
that set me apart from other Christians.
(I now try to place more emphasis
on beliefs we have in common.)

I do know that Being Catholic
is not just a matter of Being Good.
Goodness comes not from any religious practices,
but from Being Loved,
by God
and by others.

I know realize that
Being Catholic
means
Being Connected.

Our Connectedness
is most powerfully symbolized in
The Eucharist.

The Eucharist confirms that
I am not alone;
God is with us
and I only need open myself to
God's Presence
In Communion.

Our Connectedness is first
with God,
but that is only a beginning;

It is also Connectedness to Community,
Connectedness with Others
in the Body of Christ.

I do not receive sacramental bread and wine alone;
I receive it at
A Sacred Meal
with Others.

We all partake of One Sacrament,
One Body of Christ.
We become
what We Eat.

My Connectedness in the Eucharist
is a Connectedness
with all Others.

I am not alone.
I am not in Competition,
I am in Communion.

Being Catholic
means not just being concerned with
my individual salvation,
but with all Others.

It is in my relationship with Others
that I experience
the Saving Power of God.

My Faith is not a head trip,
but a heart trip;
Not a matter of ideas,
but Relationships.

My Faith is not so much concerned
with my growing in knowledge,
but more concerned with
Growing in Love.

Being Catholic
does not mean escaping or condemning the world,
it means
Fully Engaging the World,
In Love.

So, why do we spend so much time and effort
condemning and excluding Others?

Seems totally Un-Catholic.

And it clearly is not
Christlike.

Bishops of the Catholic Church,

As Faithful Catholics,
We have a Right
To Your

Understanding and Empathy,
Decisiveness,
Correct Focus,
Persistence and Follow-through
Openness, and
Disclosure.

With the Sex-abuse of our youth
by priests of the Catholic Church,
You, instead, demonstrated

Naivety about the predators and their crimes,
Insensitivity to the pain of the victims,
Disgraceful Indecisiveness in reporting the crimes,
A shameful focus on protecting the institution, not
people,
No effort at establishing National policies of
protection,
Massive efforts to cover up the facts,
Little effort to tell us what happened and why.

Isn't it time
You stepped down
To give us

The Leadership we deserve.

Catholic Education

Despite all the jocularity
about our grade-school education
by the good nuns,
I value all my Catholic Education;

St. Nicholas School (Sisters of St. Basil the Great)
Weber High School (Resurrectionist Fathers)
John Carroll University (Jesuits)
and
forty years later,
Saint Mary's University of Minnesota (Christian
Brothers)
Master of Arts in Pastoral Ministries.

And I'm still studying my religion daily.

I am convinced
Theology is an Adult Activity.

Unfortunately, Catholic Education in Theology
begins at an age when students
can't comprehend it
and
usually ends at a time
when they could begin to understand.

Most Adults are educated and Catholic,
but not Educated Catholics.

Some priests and bishops prefer it this way.
Just take a look at whom
Theology Education is focused in parishes.

Catholic Fundamentalism

In contemporary Roman Catholicism,
fundamentalists are more likely to be called
traditionalists,
and today the Vatican is their sponsor.

In addition to reading the Bible uncritically,
in search of ready answers to the problems of life,
they read papal statements that way,
finding in encyclicals the false certitude
that the Vatican warns biblical literalists against.

The most recent case in point is
Pope Benedict's recent Apostolic Exhortation.

What begins as a contemplative appreciation
of the Eucharist
ends up as a manifesto
designed to keep many Catholics from receiving
Communion at Mass.

The ticket to Communion
is an uncritical acceptance of what the pope calls,
in a striking echo,
fundamental values,
which include defense of human life from
conception to natural death.

The key declaration is that these values *are not
negotiable.*

But culture consists precisely in negotiation of values,
and change in how values are understood
is part of life.
Moral reasoning is not mere obedience,
but lively interaction among principles, situations,
and
human limitations.

Take conception.
The great Thomas Aquinas
depended on 13th-century notions of biology,
and did not believe that human life began at
conception.
Negotiation followed.

Take natural death.
Disagreements over its meaning
(including among Catholic bishops)
were made vivid not long ago
in the case of Terri Schiavo.
Negotiation followed.

The pope affirms universal and unchanging values
grounded in human nature,
as if human nature is fixed, instead of evolving.

One detects here, too, a suspicion of Darwin, an
invitation to intellectual suicide.

The various fundamentalisms are all concerned with
fortifying borders,
and that is a purpose of today's Vatican.

The pope's exhortation concludes by referring to
the Catholic people as
the flock entrusted to bishops.
Sheep stay inside the fence.

But what happens when
Catholics stop thinking of themselves as sheep?

From
JAMES CARROLL

FROM HIS BOSTON GLOBE COLUMN OF MONDAY,
MARCH 19, 2007
"THE MANY FORMS OF FUNDAMENTALISM."

Catholic, Indeed,

but same as
growing up in ethnic ghettos of Chicago
with a catholic church for each nationality?

Growing up with fear of crossing the street
before confession?

Knowing we were one True religion
and everybody else going to hell?

Memorizing ten commandments
and six precepts of the church
and thinking that was essence of our faith?

Believing priests and nuns could do no wrong?

Assuming we had a right to a free education
by unpaid nuns?

Faith was a set of dogmas cast in concrete?

Thinking Church was a building
or the priests and nuns?

Acting as if
the means were more important than the ends,
the container of our faith more important
than the contents?

Babies who died went to Limbo?
Indulgences could reduce purgatory time?

Paying, Praying, and Obeying?

Challenging

Some people I know
and Love
and Respect
feel it's wrong to challenge
the Church hierarchy.

They feel, I think, that an attack
on the human hierarchy
Is an attack on Church itself
and thus wrong.

Though they likely do not subscribe per se
to "Pay, Pray, and Obey,"
They place their trust in the power of prayer alone.

For me, True Church is much larger
than the Institution;
It is we, as the Living Body of Christ.
The Institution is human,
and though Divinely Inspired,
organized and run with free-willed humans
with human faults and frailties.

Though loss, injustice, and suffering are
a normal part of Life's Journey,
I do not believe Jesus expects
us not to speak out and act against such.

God is at work
in all of Creation,
not solely within any one institution or religion.

No one organization
has an exclusive corner on
the Truth.

There is no question that
Church hierarchy has
made mistakes,
caused suffering,
abused power.

Simply letting that continue without speaking out
cannot be what Jesus intended.

After all, he spoke out
against the errant hierarchy of His day.

Be Not Afraid

"Behind the rigid rule of Pope Benedict XVI
is a man who lives in terror
of grassroots rebellions,
says a renegade theologian
who was once his
friend.
After student revolts swept Germany in 1968,
'he got more and more conservative,
more and more frightened,'
says Hans Kung.
Pope Benedict now embraces a medieval idea
of the Catholic church,
rejecting such notions as relativism,
or the idea that nothing can ever be
absolutely right or wrong.
In contrast, Kung says,
we should be
asking: "'What would Jesus do if he were Pope?
I can't believe
He would
forbid the (birth control) pill today,
or the ordination of women.'"

Church and Change

Change for Christians
Implies
Conversion,
Metanoia,
Becoming New.

It calls us
to an Openness
to the Spirit
Who reveals Herself
in unexpected ways.

As affirmed in Vatican II,
We are Pilgrim Church
Always on the Move.

The Role of Church
is to bring about
Change in the World;

Change for Justice,
Change for Peace,
Change for Human Dignity,
Change for Freedom.

Church
is called to be,
Church Must be

The Change Agent.

Only as such can it be a Servant of God.

Church Theology
Becomes
Obsolete
Irrelevant

if it is not Re-Expressed
in the context of today's Reality.

Church, itself
becomes
Obsolete,
Irrelevant

if it is
Set in Stone.

The Word of God
is Living,
Life-Giving.

It must be
Re-Interpreted
in terms of our understanding of Life Today,
in terms of Current Scholarship.

The Church does not
Have
God
or
Grace
or
Truth,

But only is

Growing into them.

Our primary obstacle is Fear:

Fear to let go,
Fear of Unknown,
Fear of Failure,
Fear of Loss,
Fear of Alienation,

Fear of Change.

God is present in All.

Fear lacks trust that God is in our Future.

The Clergy
by St. Catherine of Siena in 1370.

More darkness and division
have come into the world
amongst the clergy of the holy church
than from any other cause.

In cases of evildoing,
they pretend not to see.

The root of self-love
is alive in them.

Because they fear to lose their position
or their temporal goods,
or their prelacy,
they . . . act like blind ones,
in that they see not the real,
so that their positions will be kept.

With a perverted hope
in their own small knowledge,
they spend so much time
in acquiring and preserving temporal things,
that they turn their back on the spiritual.

They fulfill the words:
These are blind
and
leaders of the blind
and if the blind lead the blind,
they both fall into the ditch.

Content or Container

So many Catholics,
including hierarchy,

seem obsessed with the forms and format
of their religion,
(kneeling, standing, sitting, right words, etc)
rather than
its Content,

As Richard Rohr says,
substituting Church-ianity for Christianity.

Those addicted to issues of format,
loving the container while missing the Content,
may look upon those
Living the Content of Jesus' message
(Inclusiveness, Love, Compassion, Forgiveness)
with
Awe and Inspiration

But many will view
Those trying to Live the Content
In any format
as being

dangerous, heretical, sinful, and unorthodox,

just as they did

Jesus.

Contrasts

Narrow Religion
seeks to fortify and separate.

Deep Religion
seeks to Transcend.

Deep Religion
seeks to disclose Truth of the Cosmos.

Deep Religion
involves higher levels of human development.

Deep Religion
involves the direct investigation
of experiential evidence disclosed
in higher stages of consciousness.

Dominator hierarchies
are rigid social hierarchies
that are instruments of oppression.

Actualization hierarchies
are growth hierarchies
seek the self-actualization of the individuals.

Narrow Religion
refers to mental beliefs.

Deep Religion
refers to the higher trans-personal realms
beyond mere beliefs.

Crisis

The True Crisis
with the Catholic Hierarchy
(not the Body of Christ)
is not

the sexual abuse cover-up,
financial fraud and the lack of transparency,
the shrinking number of ordained male priests,
the lack of accountability to the people,
the closing of Our churches,
sexual discrimination

though any or all of these
could spell its undoing.

The True Crisis
with the Catholic Hierarchy
(not the Body of Christ)
is
the sacrificing of spirituality for religion,
the sacrificing of the mystical for the moral,
the sacrificing of the Mission of Christ for its own
mission,
the sacrificing of Christ-given Freedoms
by domination and oppression,
the sacrificing of people for the good of an
institution,
sacrificing Truth,

which Will spell its undoing
as such.

The Cross

None of Jesus' friends called Him an ascetic.
His enemies called him a glutton and drunkard.
Today, in terms of ascetical practice,
many, so-called followers of Jesus,
strive to out-do Him.

I don't think Jesus opted for the Cross.

When He saw it before Him in Gethsemane,
He didn't run to embrace it.
Jesus didn't have a messiah complex.
He didn't play hero.

Jesus was scared—big time.
He must have experienced traumatic self-doubt.
It was His moment of truth.

As the realization of what has about to happen
to him sank in,
He likely wished He were somewhere else.
but He knew He couldn't be.

Jesus stood His ground and faced reality fully.

He could only go forward
and be nailed to the cross.

He didn't want that loathsome thing.
Who—in their right mind—would?

But Jesus could not deny who He was and
what He stood for.

So He faced the cross and it killed Him or
He allowed Himself to die on it.

I approach the cross
as I face up to who I am and to my mission
as Jesus did,
with a natural aversion,
yet facing it
and trying to accept its consequences.

My understanding of the Good News of Jesus
is that we are called to
the Fullness of Life and to the Resurrection.
On the way to The Resurrection,
my cross will intrude
in one way or another.

But I am not called to opt for it
as if it were an end in itself.

Jesus didn't opt for the cross.

When He saw that His life had brought Him to
the point of facing up to whatever it brought,
He opted, not for the cross,
but for Faithfulness to His Father.

That Loving Response
did lead to the imposition of the cross on Him,
different than Him choosing it.

I strive for Loving fidelity to God,
regardless of consequences,
always entailing some kind of sacrifice.

I think one function of prayer is to
keep me focused on
Life and Resurrection.

A spirituality that focuses on the cross,
Instead of the Resurrection,
is not life-affirming and
does not bring Joy, only fear and depression.

I'm not much into the cross,
certainly do not feel "called to it."

A spirituality that sees only the Resurrection,
with never a cross in sight,
is shallow and unreal.

I need to keep my eyes on both,

But with both my ears
attuned to the True Call:

Resurrection.

Theology and Dialogue

Connection and Dialogue,
so fundamental to Christianity,
(Jesus was constantly in Dialogue with Others)
is strangely missing in today's Catholicism.

Theology is born through Questions
that are asked by contemporaries and
one must start by Listening
before proclaiming summaries of long ago.

The Quest for Truth pre-supposes Dialogue.

The tentative Dialogue of Vatican II
did not last long.
And the poor dialogue has resulted in
poor theology.

We see this with the present hierarchy
where the paramount concern is
preservation of the institution,
A theological crisis!

The bad theology we oft hear on Sundays
compounds the problem.

We have had bold and prophetic theologians
Who re-think and re-formulate Faith
for today and tomorrow,
but they have paid a high price:
threatened, sacked, exiled, silenced.

We have bad theology because of
the ruling structures of the church,
who take little account of theologians
and make a narrow orthodoxy
the measure of loyalty.

They confuse thirst
with relativism
and continue to launch anathemas,
forbidding new thoughts
of the poetry of theological work.

Good theology,
the basis of a healthy church,
is humans taking hold of
the Word of God,
kneading it,
shaping it into human words and images,
baking it in the fire of critical dialogue,
so that it can be received as
the bread of life
by ALL God's people.

It cannot be
the voice of only one group
of the human family,
as it needs the full range of human experience,
including the voice of the poor and rich,
females and males,
lay people and ordained.

The difference between PRIESTHOOD and ORDINATION
is very important to the life of the Church today.

Priesthood is a calling.
God is the one who does the calling.
God may call whomever God wills.

It's hard for people to discern God
and accurately interpret God's callings.
So wise and humble people
bring their spiritual perceptions of
God's callings in important matters
to their spiritual community of faith,
to lay their experience before others
and seek assistance to best discern
what God may be saying to them,
calling them to do.
The goal is to discern the truth
regarding the call,
then, having done the best possible
to discern the truth,
to surrender oneself to God's will,
however that needs to happen,
given the nature of the calling.

Discernment ultimately is the responsibility
not of the community
but of the one called.

However, because of our human propensities
to deceive ourselves,

it happens best
with the assistance of the spiritual gifts of
discernment
in the faith community.

(Only the one called can discern and respond.)

The Church ordains.
Ordination is a way for humans to express that
they believe the calling is valid,
to commit support to the vocation of the one called,
and challenge the called one
to live out the calling with integrity.

By establishing various sieves,
the Church has chosen not to consider
ordination of various categories of people
who feel called.
The sieve process bypasses
the entire process of discernment
for the selected populations.
It is assumed "God doesn't call these people".
If one of these people experiences a call to
priesthood, therefore, it must be an illusion.
There used to be prohibitions
against ordaining anyone with a physical handicap.
(They were a "blemished offering to the Lord."
This Levitical theology has been gradually
disappearing.)

The Church's sieves presently summarily exclude
the married and the female.
Only single men make it through the sieve.

It is NOT true that "There are not enough PRIESTS".
God has promised to provide
what God's people need.
"Every hair on your head is counted."
"You are worth more than a sparrow."

God provides us with an abundant supply of PRIESTS.
The world is full of priestly single and married women,
and priestly married men.

However, the Church has simply chosen
to no longer be a discerning community of faith,
to no longer abandon itself humbly to the process of
discerning God's will and following it.
It is no longer willing to be seriously engaged
in the process of working with anyone
who experiences a call from God,
to spiritually discern the truth of their call,
and then honor God's work in that person
(then integrating a human process of validation,
training, support, and living in integrity with the call,
through seminary training and
post-ordination support for growth
and development).

So the Church has thousands of priests
that exist in God's mind and in God's call,
but not in the active, ordained service of the Church.

The Church does not have enough
ORDAINED PRIESTS
due to its unwillingness to ordain all those
whom God calls.

In this way, the Church has chosen
to no longer be a partner with the Holy Spirit
in nurturing the life of the Church.
This is a serious matter.
Scripture says, "Do not grieve the Holy Spirit."

This act of choosing to not even consider the
possibility of a valid call to priesthood
to thousands of men and women worldwide,
to work with them in good faith
in the process of spiritual discernment,
and to ordain those whom God has called,
must certainly grieve the Holy Spirit.

In the work of guiding souls
one learns that,
when the heart is committed to God,
moving WITH God's will brings peace and ease,
a sense of life energy flowing with the current,
even if that peace is beyond
our rational understanding,
spiritual calm is in the midst of emotional pain,
and what we are doing
moves against the current
of destructive human activity around us.

When we move AGAINST God's will,
we feel a sense of unsettledness, of anxiety,
of "going against the grain",
"swimming against the current",
of a subtle wrongness, dis-ease,
even when we are surrounded by
what we think should make us happy.

Is this why our Church leaders are so full of fear?
And our Church so often feels anxious, and lifeless?

Are we corporately moving against God's will
in this matter,
and suffering the effects of corporate sin,
due to leadership decisions to act against God's will
for the Church,
due to the sinful desire of men
to cling to the exercise of institutional power?

If we actually desire what we pray --
that "Thy will be done" --
then we will actually see the will of God taking place
before us....

God's will is for us to flourish,
and for all his priestly people to live out their callings,
as he has charged them.
We will see the death of the disobedient Church,
because it is causing its own spiritual death.

And we will see the obedient Church come to life,
because God honors obedience to his will --
even with miracles.

By

Barbara M. DeGrand

Discovery/Confession

I've been critical of
conservative Catholics
for being museum keepers
and
for being frozen in the past

when

I discover that,
in my futile efforts to help reform Church,
I am just as guilty,
by my letting the Institution define Catholicism
for me,
rather than

Jesus Christ.

Jesus was not bound by the hierarchy of His time,
why have I been letting the hierarchy of my time
contain my idea of
True Catholicism.

Jesus' life and message were
inclusive, disruptive, and non-bureaucratic;
Did I really think

the Institution of today

could be the same?

Distinguishing Characteristics of Jesus' Teachings

A sense of urgency
An ardent, vivid quality
An abandon

His "Invitational" style
Working with peoples' imagination more than reason
An invitation to "See things" differently

Grounded

Located Authority, not in Himself, not in God
removed,
but in our own hearts.

Contra-conventional wisdom:
World: Resist evil; **Jesus**: Turn other cheek,
W: Love Friends, Hate enemies: **J**: Love Your Enemies,
W: Be Discriminating; **J**: Sun rises on Just and Unjust
alike,
W: Respectable people up front;
J: Outcasts and Harlots enter first,
W: Wide gate to Heaven; **J**: Narrow,
W: Be Prudent; **J**: Be as Carefree as birds and flowers,
W: Wealth is important;
J: Camel through Eye of Needle,
W: Rich will be Happy; **J**: Not so

Always coming back to
God's overwhelming Love of Humanity
and
the need for people to accept that Love.

That Blessedness is not unalloyed happiness,
where sorrow is eliminated,
but indeed,

Paradoxical Happiness
where sorrow is not eliminated,
but
Enfolded and Transmuted
by
God's all-permeating Love.

Embrace Confusion!

Mary and Joseph
must have been totally confused
by events that seemed to overtake their lives.

Jesus
never seems to answer so much
as confuse
with His parables.

Mary Magdalene's
entire history
seems one of Confusion.

The whole post-crucifixion
Resurrection
sequence of events
is totally confusing to the participants.

A belief in absolute answers
to un-answerable questions,
and one that demands
proof of the un-provable,
deals in magic

rather than

The Mystery
of
True Christianity.

Of Miters and Minutiae

Emphasizing adherence to liturgical minutiae

to the neglect of authentic gospel living

may bring an illusion of unity

but will never yield authentic faith.

The Vatican

and

its Bishops

are trying to keep the Titanic from sinking

by re-arranging the silverware

in its ever-emptying

dining hall.

Essential Messages of Vatican II

The Mission of Church
Is no longer to be exclusively focused on
Preparing individuals
To attain eternal life;
But rather on
Witnessing to God's Love and Compassion
By bringing
Justice and Healing to the world
Here and Now.

Modernity
Is no longer viewed with
Suspicion and antagonism
But rather with
Critical Sympathy
And
Engagement.
Church is to
Share
The Joys, Hopes, Grief, and Anguish of the age,
Rather than view them from afar.

Church now fosters
A Positive attitude towards
Other branches of Christianity.
Church needs reform,
Values Scripture,
Heeds the Call of the Laity,
And
Supports Collegial structures in Church governance.

Prickly Apartness Is Dead.

An Ethical/Moral Sexuality

Respects Autonomy
Requires Free Consent of both parties
Respects Bodily Integrity
Tells Truth
Keeps Promises

Involves Mutual Participation
Calls for Active Participation by Both

Demands Equality of Power
Treats neither as a commodity

Requires some sense of Commitment
Needs an enduring Love
Results in Growth of Both Parties

Is Fruitful
Is Inclusive, not exclusive
Takes responsibility for Offspring

Commands Respect
Is based on Social Justice
Calls for Security and Social Justice

Can only heterosexuals have this moral relationship?

Eucharist as Communion

Eucharist
is supposed to have a Transforming effect
on us.

Eucharist is supposed to send us forth
determined to do something.

Eucharist is supposed to
change our priorities.

Many prefer a docile, consoling Eucharist.

Many see it as a product
for personal consumption.

John Paul II proclaimed that
Eucharist fosters Social Love,
seeking Common Good
over private food.

And yet,
Vatican pronouncements
and upcoming documents
concentrate on

Eucharist as object of adoration.

The Vatican approach
is one-sided, discouraging, and
totally inadequate.

"The Eucharist:
Source and Summit
of the Life and Mission of the Church"
is preoccupied with

ceremonial propriety.

The Vatican
overemphasizes adoration
vs. Service

and an individualistic link
between believer and Jesus.

Lost by the Vatican
is St. Augustine's plea
to partake of Christ's body
to become Christ's body in the world.

Lost by the Vatican
is the intimate connection
between Eucharist
and Service.

Dioceses
are promoting Eucharistic adoration
as never before.

A few churches
expose the Eucharist sparingly
because their pastors
want parishioners to see
that they are tabernacles of Christ.

The Vatican emphasis
tends to provide people
a place to hide
from the cares of the world.

Once again,
the Vatican
is out of touch
with the real world,
and
has got it wrong.

Eucharist IS Communion.

Faith

My Faith
must be

Vibrantly Expressed
(even though all won't agree)

Critically Examined
(willing to grow out of conventional wisdom)

and

Ultimately Transformed
(despite institutional resistance to change)

Religions have sacrificed the Mystical for the moral;
They should be about Transformation,

not boundaries.

Faith, Hope, and Love

Many of the actions by the hierarchy
of the Catholic Church
seem inconsistent with the Life and Message of Jesus,

but I have **Faith** that this church will be Re-Formed.

Re-Formation of the Church
cannot be achieved in a lifetime,
so I just **Hope**
that the Holy Spirit continues to guide us
through the change.

A Re-Formation of the Church
cannot be accomplished by individuals,
so I draw on **Love** to unite us
and
provide the Energy it requires.

Fear drives out Love

Over the years,
with the help of the Holy Spirit,
I have been able to
Help Bereaved move along their Grief Journeys,
Assist Caregivers in becoming more effective,
and
Guide Life's Seekers in nurturing their Spirituality.

Much of this Ministry
has taken place in a diocese
which now has become
totally oppressive
and
fear-driven.

Although the people and parishes
to whom I have ministered over the years
have expressed gratitude, appreciation,
and recommendation,

Fear has driven out Love.

In addition to ministering to
Grievers, Caregivers, and Spiritual Travelers,
I have been totally and unabashedly outspoken
against the evils and ills
of Institutional Church.

Many dissenters have been penalized,
and have paid the price.

In numerous dioceses across the country
for Speaking the Truth,
with a number in this diocese
even losing their jobs.

But it is unfortunate in this instance,
that by keeping my ministry and gifts
from those who might benefit from it,
I am not the one penalized.

For this, I am sorry.

And to those who are instruments of this separation,
I pray that you let
Love drive out the fear
which seems to rule your hearts today.

The Catholic Church:
Last feudal system in the West.

Once the feudal structure of the church
is recognized,
the bishops' response to the clergy abuse crisis
comes into focus.

Bishops and other church authorities
reacted to the scandal
the only way their feudal culture allowed
with secrecy, denial,
and a no-holds-barred effort
to protect the reputation, authority,
and resources of the institution.

While tragic-and in many cases reprehensible,
Their response was consistent
with the way feudal systems function.

The laity must now bring about
accountability and transparency
to the current difficulties of the church.

American Catholics,
among the best-educated
and responsive laity in the world,
need to assert their dignity and responsibility
as full, equal and adult members of the church.

The laity must find their voice
but also to dare to speak to church authorities
long accustomed to deferential obedience
and compliance.

The church will never,
Thank God,
be the same.

Much is at stake at this time:
the sacramental character of the church;
its mission of liberation in the way of Jesus;
the role of the laity and particularly of women;
the future of ministry;
and the church's structures of governance.

The feudalism,
from which the church still suffers,
is described by historians as
an economic, political and social system
based on land, loyalty and the need for security
and protection.
Its linchpin is unquestioned loyalty.

It is difficult to justify such a system in our current
world.

What is needed more so in today's world
is the humility to listen to each other
and
to oneself in honesty.

It is important to know that
not only do American Catholics
listen with their hearts and souls;
they also listen with well-educated minds.

On any given Sunday,
a priest may find at the Mass he is offering,
men and women with graduate degrees
in theology or Scripture.

They want to listen but
also to be heard.

Looking back at the first centuries of the church,
prior to the regulation of celibacy,
approximately a dozen popes in the first millennium
were sons of priests.

Adrian II
(867-872) was the last married pope
but Pope John XV (985-986) was the son of a priest.

Is there room, then,
for discussion
of such topics as celibacy in the church?

There are currently more priests in their 90's
than under 35.

The competence and commitment
of many lay leaders in the church,
as well as in secular life,
who continue the liberation of the laity
initially inspired by Vatican II.

The exercise of authority without accountability
Is not servant leadership;
it is tyranny.

And this scandal, paradoxically,
has liberated American Catholics
perhaps more than any other impetus.

Church leaders can be Church leaders
only to the extent that they themselves follow Christ.

We need to examine the fears that breed mistrust
and suspicion
among the various factions of the church.

What is it that we fear will be lost?

We can ignore such questions
only at the peril of the integrity of the Church
founded by Christ.

Freedom

Jesus gifted us with Freedom.

As He stated in His Sermon on the Mount,
Through Love,
We can be free from
Worldly securities,
The Need for constant pleasure,
Power, control and approval,
Conventional wisdom,
Over-identification with a group,
Our hurts,
Lack of forgiveness,
Our minds,
Results,
and Self possessiveness.

Yet, Institutions
even Church
try and take away
these Christ-given gifts.

They encourage us to

Find Security outside ourselves, in them,
Relinquish power and control to them,
Rely on their wisdom,
Identify totally with them,
Seek forgiveness through them,
Keep it mental,
but not think for ourselves.

Who gave these institutions the right
to take away

Our Gift of Freedom?

What made us so weak-kneed
to relinquish

Our Gift of Freedom?

Freedom and Spirituality

The Freedom of the Children of God
proclaimed by the Gospel in many ways
is today being transgressed
within our community of faithful itself.

Oh, the Laity of the Church are active,
but to be active
and to be Free
are not the same.

The Laity, for the most part,
do not know of their oppression,
and would deny it
if argued in their presence.

The worst form of oppression,
Spiritual,
is one in which
the captives have been induced
to embrace their own oppression.

This structural oppression
limits the freedom of
the entire Faith Community,
including the leadership,
who find it the hardest
to think outside the box.

This is not about Laity vs. Clergy.

The structural changes
required of Church
come best from below,
from those are least invested in
maintenance of the present structure.

I oft fretted

about how my kids were living their lives,

albeit good ones,

outside the Church,

at least the Church as I defined it,

or a Church as its hierarchy defined it.

In answering Jesus' call

to think and live "outside the box,"

as taught us in His parables,

I have humbly learned

that my Kids, after all,

have NOT been living their lives outside the Church

as Jesus would have defined it,

[had he thought it important enough to define.]

Forgive me, Kids,

for being so long stuck in conventional wisdom's
myopic idea of Church

and for not heeding Jesus' True call

to a Church that mirrored His life,

Inclusive, Disruptive, and Non-bureaucratic,

one who's mission is Love

and not perpetuation of an institution.

From Religion to Spirituality

Official religions
are not providing convincing answers
to Faith Questions
or
more importantly
are not even addressing Faith Questions.

The statements of Christian belief
such as the Creeds
are couched in a language of a past age
not addressing
the everyday world
in which we Live.

Institutional religions
no longer convince people
they are the sole possessors
of Truth.

Many of us have been forced to look elsewhere.

In looking elsewhere,
We discover people of Other Faiths
living in our midst
and we recognize their Goodness.

What is Life all about?

In the past,
Institutional religions controlled
our thought processes.
No more.

We seek a Spirituality which is
holistic, non-dogmatic, and self-improving.

Institutional religions seem
out-dated, irrelevant, and conflict-causing.

Gay Priests

A young Catholic priest in full cassock
stands before a black backdrop
gripping a cross in one hand and a rosary
in the other.
A halo of light surrounds him,
but his expression is far from angelic.
He stares grimly at the ground, his eyes obscured
by dark sunglasses.

Over the last three years of
the clergy sex abuse crisis,
priests have come to be identified
with the dark side of human behavior.

Bishops have responded by absolving themselves
and
transforming their child protection policies
while removing accused clergy from church work.

And now, Vatican-directed evaluators
have started visiting all American seminaries,
looking for lapses in teaching about celibacy.

A document from the Vatican directs evaluators
to look for "evidence of homosexuality" in seminaries.
Meanwhile, the Vatican is expected to soon release
a document
signaling that **gays are not welcome in seminaries.**

Why cannot celibate, gay priests serve the church?

Can the Church revive a dying profession by making it even more chauvinistic,
more exclusive?
(Did Christ enlist an elitist cadre in His time?)

It is amazing that there are any young men
who are willing to sign up these days .

Since 1965, the number of annual ordinations has dropped by more than half and
enrollment in graduate-level seminaries has dropped from 8,300 to 3,300 in the same period.

Thousands of parishes are without a resident priest and the average age of Catholic clergy is high and climbing.

The priesthood is also experiencing orthodoxy gap.
Younger priests tend to be more conservative,
viewing themselves as **higher in holiness than the laity**
and as **"upholders of the faith,"**
rather than as servants working to benefit broader society.

This same gulf exists in some seminaries
between progressive faculty
and their conservative students.

Vatican evaluators will ask
if faculty members accept Catholic teaching
and whether the school has a process
for removing those who don't.

The Vatican is concerned that some seminaries
are maintaining a certain laxity about sexual morality
distorting the perspective of would-be priests,
who would get the impression
that the church is not entirely serious
about its moral teachings.

The abuse crisis refocused Vatican attention
on gay priests,
since most abuse victims were adolescent boys
even while experts on sex offenders
say homosexuals are no more likely than
heterosexuals
to molest young people.

But that did not stifle the Vatican search for
homosexual seminarians.
It is maintained that gay subcultures in seminaries
are alienating heterosexuals,
prompting them to drop out.

Estimates of the number of gays in seminaries
and the priesthood
range from 25 percent to 50 percent.

It is unclear what action if any the Vatican will take
after evaluators finish their inspections.
But gay priests say it is naive to think that seminaries
will suddenly fill up
if homosexuals are banished.

The single biggest deterrent to recruitment
Is not homosexuality,
but mandatory celibacy.

If celibacy were optional for diocesan priests,
there would be an estimated fourfold increase in
seminarians.

So why the hunt for gay seminarians?

And what of all the gay priests

now serving the people of God?

Getting Our Church Back on Mission

Getting Institutional Church
back to the Mission of Jesus
can never happen
if it is left to the clergy,
or even to specially trained lay ministers.

We cannot pay others
to do it for us.

We have to do it ourselves.

Else we fail as followers of Jesus
and the Church fails in its fundamental mission,
to live the gospel.

Living the gospel
does not mean
memorizing Bible passages or
attending prayer meetings,
memorizing the catechism or
going to Mass.

It does not mean
having the answers and going to church,
but
Living the Answer and Being Church.

It does not mean
simply obeying the commandments
(old testament morality)
but
Enjoying the Beatitudes.

It is not possible
to live the life of Jesus alone;
That is why we must Be Church,
Be the Body of Christ.

If the Institution is to be renewed in our day,
it must be in our Living the gospel
and being Good News

despite the rules.

God to ALL for ALL

(from a homily by Bishop Thomas Gumbleton)

Jesus came as a Jew. He lived as a Jew.

He died as a Jew -- never having set up a Church--

only calling together a community of disciples

to carry on his Word.

But then there too it began to happen again

what happened with the Chosen People.

There were those who began to say,

"No, it's exclusive -- only Christians.

Only those who explicitly acknowledge Jesus

as the Savior will be saved."

But Paul is saying, "No, the Good News is different."

And in fact, that's what we learn in the Gospel.

The people who came to adore Jesus,

as Matthew described it,

were from the East

which would have meant, perhaps,

the country of Iraq or the country of Iran,

which at that point was Persia.

They were probably seers of some sort or priests.

Many people think of the Zoroastrian religion.

They came and they went back praising God.

This is ALL to show us that Jesus came

not just for the Chosen People,

not just for those who call themselves Christian

but for ALL people.

They didn't change their religion when they left.

They were still Zoroastrian priests.

God had entered into human history for EVERYONE.

That's the same thing that you discover if you listen
carefully to what Isaiah was saying.

God promising, "Nations will come to your light, kings

to the brightness of your dawn.

Lift up your eyes roundabout

and see they are ALL gathered and come to you.

This sight will make your face radiant,

your heart throbbing and full.

The riches of the sea will return to you,

the wealth of the nations will come to you."

Then he goes on to describe

how people will come "from Midian and Ephah.

Those from Sheba will come bringing with them

gold and incense."

People coming from everywhere,

returning to the Promised Land

to rebuild for the Jewish people their Temple,

their Kingdom.

But again the message is so clear –

God came, in Jesus, for EVERYONE

and ALL share in this great Good News.

Not just a few of us but EVERYONE.

It seems that somehow –

every religion probably does this to some extent --
people begin to think,

"I have the truth.

We have the truth.

No one else has the truth.

We have the whole truth.

You must believe like we believe or you're not faithful
to God."

God speaks to ALL in various ways.

Those Zoroastrian priests somehow

through lights in the heavens began to discover
God.

People of other religious traditions today

discover God in their own way –

God working in and through them

and their religious traditions.

We cannot narrow it down

so that only a few will know the truth, have the truth.

We find truth in ALL religions.

And, of course, if we rarely accepted that,

we would not have religious wars

Christians going into the Middle East

to destroy the Muslims

who had taken over part of that area.

We would not be threatened with religious wars,

if only we would understand that God's ways
are not our ways,

God's thoughts are not our thoughts.

God's ways and God's thoughts

are as far above our ways and our thoughts

as the heavens are above the earth.

We always try to narrow it down.

Make God's ways our ways,

but they're not.

God acts outside and beyond any religious tradition.

The spirit of God moves where it will.

So we can find truth in other religions.

And we need to understand that and accept that

and respect that

we are ALL brothers and sisters in the human family;

ALL sons and daughters of God.

We need to understand that and accept it

so that we begin, each of us, ALL of us,

to have a greater respect for others.

If we begin to understand

that God is alive and present in ALL people,

in ALL religious traditions,

then we must respect each other.

So there is a very real challenge for us.

We must respect and revere and have high regard
for the truth
that we discover in other religious traditions and
respect the people who are Muslims,
who are Jews,
who are Hindus,
whatever,
but we also have to try to be faithful
to what we say we are -- followers of Jesus Christ.
When we are fully faithful to that,
then the Good News that Paul is talking about
will break forth in ever greater clarity.
God's love will break forth into our world
because we act as the Light of the Nations.
We bring the goodness,
the love,
the care of Jesus into our whole human family
as Jesus intended it.
ALL of us are brothers and sisters.
Every person on the earth is a son or daughter of
God.
Among them we try to be a light as Jesus leads us
and guides us
to bring the fullness of God's love into our world.

Grumpiness

There seems to be a correlation between someone's implied ecclesiology

and their overall attitude toward

the Catholic church.

More often than not, when people complain about "the church"

no matter what their ideological

or theological slant,

whether they're inside the church or outside,

what they mean is the hierarchy or clergy.

Sometimes it's actually just a handful of members of the hierarchy or clergy

whom they find especially irritating.

This sort of "purple ecclesiology,"

seeing the church almost exclusively

in terms of the clergy

is a prescription for grumpiness.

The happiest Catholics seem to have a much broader concept of "church,"

whether they're conscious of it or not.

For them, "the church" is a vast universe

of individuals, movements, parishes, schools, journals, international networks,

and all manner of other slices of life,

engaged in a dizzying variety of activities,

from contemplative prayer to feeding the hungry,

to striving to translate the gospel

into art, politics, finance, medicine,

and other realms of secular culture.

For those who see the church this way,

whatever their political or theological positions ,

the clergy may play an important role,

but command relatively little of their energy

and imagination.

For every aspect of "the church"

that they find frustrating or disappointing,

such Catholics can usually reel off

dozens of other things they find encouraging.

Heresy

People are excommunicated,
not for sins of morality,
but for sins of heresy.

The New Testament Greek word for heresy,
hairetikos,
translated by church
as a belief opposed to orthodox doctrine,
in fact, literally means
"able to choose,"
a capacity unwelcome
in institutional religion.

There seems to come a point
in a person's life
when a bishop's threat of excommunication
cannot muffle
God's call.

All Christians are Christ-bearers.

The Hierarchy

The loss of credibility by our Church leaders
over the clergy sex abuse and financial dealings
casts doubt on what they say
and even taints their good works.

By their silence and cover-up they have lost our trust.
What makes this particularly distressful is that they
seem relatively unchanged by it.
"This too, shall pass", seems to be their philosophical
response.
Even their words of sorrow are suspect
because there is no evidence of repentance
or change.

It is business as usual.

The fall-out from these catastrophic events
is yet to be fully understood.

More and more we must now trust the voice of our
own conscience
together with the common sense
of the community
BEFORE we defer to those who claim spiritual
authority.

We have learned from sad experience
that they are flawed,
especially when it comes to sex and money.

We know it, they know it,
and the whole world knows it.

The Truths of our faith remain the same.

The Creed we profess has not changed.

The Church remains.
But those in whom we trusted to guide us have
demonstrated their humanity.

Forgive them?
Certainly,
just as we seek forgiveness for our own humanness.

But can we trust their judgments?
Experience dictates otherwise.

Consider the range of decisions rendered by
our all-too-male-celibate guides
and ponder how their answers
may have been tainted by their humanity.

The Catholic sensus fidelium differs from their
teachings on many issues.
Answers based on lived faith
and experience of the community
and the growing understanding of our
Christian traditions are better ways
of knowing and living God's will for us.

We will always have leaders and experts with us,
but faith in the Christian community, as a good and
Spirit-filled guide, has been restored to its primacy.

As it was from the beginning,
our Church leaders are to give priority
to the Spirit-filled voice of the community
over their own personal views
(not like Paul VI in Humanae Vitae)
before they open their mouth to teach.

This is probably the best fallout
(and most feared by Rome),
and could be consider as a special gift
of the Spirit
to help us heal.

(From a document by ARCC (http://arcc-catholic-rights.net/temple_site.htm))

Hope to Women in the Church

The Document
The Church in the Modern World
(Gaudium et Spes)
from
Vatican II

provides Hope for
All Women in the Church.

Its message is grounded in
the Inalienable Dignity of the Human Person
created in the Image of God.

Human Dignity, Freedom, Community,
Equality of All Persons, and Social Justice
Are all rooted in
Man and Woman created in God's image.

It sees the Church
at the Service of Humanity.

Women are called,
not just to serve the family,
but to Service of the world.

It encourages Dialogue.

It is vital for the world
and greatly desired by the Church
that the two meet,
get to know each other,
and Love one another.
(Pope Paul VI)

Gaudium et Spes
called all Men and Women
to see oneself as God's image,
as Servants of the world,
and Partners in Dialogue.

Is it any wonder
those males who wish to keep control
would bury Gadium et Spes
and all of Vatican II with it.

Ignore the Bad because of the Good?

The many good deeds and works of Catholic
Charities and Catholic Relief Services
do not justify
the oppressive violence or arrogant insular archaic
attitudes of the Roman hierarchy.

The Church total character must be weighted
against
the whole behavior and attitudes,
as is said in contemporary moral theology.

While its works for justice and peace
are tremendously laudable,
they don't make up for the considerable
overwhelming damage
done with reactionary protectionist
demeaning attitudes
toward other believers and their faith,
Christian or other faiths.

Such oppression, violence, and injustice
must be challenged
even when surrounded by some good works.

Take the pole out of your eye,
see clearly the negative impact of the corporate
status quo dogma structures
of the Roman corporate model of Church.

Impediments to Spiritual Growth

The rift between
Religion and Eros

Religion gets to keep God;
The Secular, Sex.

The Secular got Passion;
Religion, chastity.

Religion in our churches today is
Anti-erotic, Anti-sex, Anti-creative, Anti-enjoyment,
and
Anti-this-world.

God is perceived as
Stoic, Celibate, Dull, Cold, Otherworldly, and
threatened by sex and human creativity.

The rift between
Spirituality and Ecclesiology

As the numbers of persons participating in churches
has decreased,
the numbers of persons interested in Spirituality
has increased.

Amidst a Spiritual renaissance,
Church life is declining.

On a True Spiritual Quest,
One never arrives;
One can not claim to be on a Spiritual Quest
settling into the practice of a religion.
Some want church, but not Faith,
Many find True Spirituality
Beyond Church.

The rift between
Morality and Social Justice

Private and Social Morality are rarely found
in the same person.

True Spirituality is about Both;
Liberality and Piety,
Contemplation and Action,
Private Morality and Social Justice.

Sadly, today, they seem divorced.

The rift between
The Gifted Child and the Giving Adult in Us

True Spirituality is about
Self-Transcendence, Altruism, and Selflessness.

The way these are taught in religions is often
Self-serving and Manipulative.

Persons who sacrifice themselves for others,
because they are afraid to disappoint,
end up bitter, feeling victimized, and angry.

The rift between
Contemporary Culture and Religion

We feel betrayed;
We expect religion to be handing down to us
The Sweetness of Life,
not false prohibitions, bitter taboos, and needless
fears.
Religion feels betrayed by its children
who judge it harshly.

We children accuse religion

of dealing us death, not life.

The Journey of John of the Cross

John met a nun twice his age,
Theresa of Avila.

She invited him to Radial Renewal
of the religious community.

John saw God's handwriting in her request
and responded with a whole-hearted Yes.

John's own religious community,
suspicious of his reforms,
imprisoned him.

For nine months,
John was held captive
in a tiny, dark, damp cell,
a former bathroom.
He was given sustenance
three times a week.

John found grace
even in that dreadful environment
and allowed it to become
his sanctuary
in which he communed with God
and composed his Love Poetry.

After six months,
John received pen and paper
from a compassionate jailer
and composed his great works,
The Spiritual Canticle
and
The Dark Night.

John was able to recognize God's Plan
in the midst of
this darkest time of his life.

The verses John composed
in the darkness of his jail cell
became the springboard for his
Spiritual Theology.

John showed us all that
God is only Here and Now
not somewhere off
in the distant future.

Knock on any Door

Knock and it shall be opened to you.

But which door?
Door number One?
Door number Two?
Door number Three?

The First Door, the Upper Door
seems too high for me.
To approach God through the upper door
is to encounter God On High,
The Transcendent God, completely Other.
This door leads to
the Holy Place
where the Most High dwells.
It opens onto
The Mountain Top
beyond
the Cloud of the Unknowing.

Maybe in time . . .

Door number two,
The Middle Door,
opens
The Way to
The Discovery of God
in the World—
In People,
In Events,
In Nature,
In the Universe.

It is the Portal of
Sensitivity to Beauty,
and
The Passageway to
Compassionate Action and
Social Justice.

It is the Door
that opens to
The Spouse,
The Child,
The Relation,
The Friend,
The Companion,
The Neighbor,
The Prisoner,
The Stranger,
The Sick,
The Hungry,
The Thirsty.
Passage Through This Door
is by
The Incarnation.

To Traverse using the Third Door,
The Lower Door,
is to Journey
Within Myself
in order to
Meet God
Within my Soul.
It is to discover
The Divine Spark,
The Spirit of God Abiding and Life-Giving.

It is to descend to
that place within me
where
The Word Dwells
With The Father
and
The Spirit.

Door One, Two, or Three,

Indeed.

Looking Back to See Forward

I look back on my business career
with
Ford Motor Company
and recall a Company Healthy and Vibrant
for its time.

But as times and the environment changed,
that organization, apparently, did not,
at least not quickly enough,
and
now suffers through major re-structuring
if it hopes to survive
and serve the needs of Customers.

Failing to meet the needs of its clients
in an effective manner
will spell doom for that organization.

It must change.

I look back at my life
with
Institutional Church
and recall an organization that
served the needs of its immigrant uneducated laity.

But as times and the environment
and the laity itself changed . . .

Losing God

Shock!

I must lose God;
at least the God I thought I knew.
The God I thought I knew
cannot be God
as God really is,
because God is Infinite
and my finite mind cannot comprehend
God.

My childhood images of God
I left behind
quite naturally.
The Old Man with a beard,
The Loving Father,
The Stern Teacher.

Along the way,
I knew
A demanding God,
A Loving God,
A Compassionate God,
A Guide.

None of these describe God.

God is these,
but
NOT ONLY THESE.
If so limited,
God would not be God.

My images of God
surely were
False Gods.

Losing my images of God
is
Unsettling.

Now I must Unlearn God,
stripping myself of the false images,
Without Putting Anything in their place.
I must Unlearn God.
I must Unknown God.

"He" is wrong.
'She" is wrong.
"It" is wrong.

Why must I Unknow God?

Because I cannot possibly Know God.

So, I come face to face with a Void.

Terrifying!

Yes,

God is No Thing.

God is Beginning
and
End.

I will not understand this,
Until I face the Void,
Enter it,
Cross it.

That takes an Heroic Act of Trust.

Divinity is totally
Incomprehensible
Utterly Other.

I need not be afraid.

Jesus is the bridge
across the Void
to
God.

Mystery

Religion is in the mystery business.
If there were no mystery in the world,
there would be no need for religion.
One must wonder then why
on both the left and the right,
there is so much effort
to take the mystery out of religion,
to reduce it either to rules taken out of context
from the scripture
or to explanations which theologians think
will persuade those influenced by science
that religion is not absurd.

Religion is indeed absurd,
but only because our existence is absurd.
How come we're here, anyway?
How come there is anything at all, anyway?
Religion is a cautious attempt to respond to mystery
with something better than the suspicion
that it is a tale told by an idiot,
full of sound and fury and signifying nothing,
if only with the modest,
"there is something afoot in the universe,
something that looks like gestation and birth."

Religion is the unpretentious affirmation
in the face of substantial contrary evidence
that God is not mad
and ask why She seems to know
so much higher math.

It is the attempt to face the odd fact that
the evolutionary process has produced minds
that are capable of comprehending
(if just barely) both General Relativity
and Quantum Theory,
when there was no advantage
in our evolutionary past of having such an intellect.

Religion is finally a tentative response to the question,
"how come, anyway?"
Many theologians, still a little breathless and a little
late,
think that science is in the process
of eliminating mystery.

When *the answer* is found
we will not be able to understand it.
Nonetheless it is clear
that the more we know about reality
the more mysterious it seems.

Only those who want to use the bible
to explain away mystery
or those who think that's what religion does
(not without some reason)
can imagine there is a conflict
between science and religion
when in fact both of them bump their heads
against the solid wall of mystery
and increasingly both think they hear murmurs
of one kind or another
from beyond that wall.

Religion therefore must be open (once again?)
to mystery.
It is a mistake in our religious services
to eliminate all openness to the marvelous,
the wonderful, the surprising,
to dispense with the poetic,
the imaginative,
the metaphorical dimensions of religion,
to exclude its experiential and the narrative aspects,
to forget that religion is poetry
and story
before it is anything else and after everything else.

The search for religious experience
and for the meaning of religious experience
seems to have increased.
Religious experience may have become
disconnected with prosaic religion
and therefore much of the search
is for links between religion and experience
which were once more obvious.

Clergy persons seem to assume
that their congregations are completely spirit-less
and that it is their function to reshape them
in the clergy person's own image and likeness
so that they give the same answers
to questions we propose
and which they are unlikely to ever ask on their own.

In fact religious experience is endemic in our society,
most of it part of and the result of ordinary
experiences of life
and almost none of it drug-induced.

The Holy is everywhere,
even if people don't know who (or Who) it is.
Religion arises from experiences
of the Holy
and takes its raw power from such experiences.

Religion is poetry before it is prose
because poetry is inevitable in telling stories
about the experience of mystery.
Yet religious leaders think that it is their job
to replace poetry with prose,
to clarify the experiential with the propositional,
and to explain stories immediately
and thus explain them away.
It seems to me that it is the task of clergy persons
to listen to their people
as they tell stories of their experiences of the Holy,
their explorations into mystery
and then to correlate their stories
with the overarching stories of the Heritage,
often through community ritual.
The emphasis here is on listening,
on keeping our mouths shut,
and on resisting the almost incurable temptation
to stretch the stories
on to our theological categories.

Why, I wonder, are we so afraid of mystery?
Why are so eager to budget the Holy Spirit's time
for Her
when on the record She is determined to blow
whither she will?

I am not asserting that reason and reflection
should be abandoned.
We are reflecting creatures.
We need doctrines and catechisms and creeds,
theologies
(even, in limited amounts, theologians),
and even some kind of teaching authority.
We must go through our critical period
between the first and the second naiveté.
We must not fixate,
as clergy and theologians often seem to do,
between the two naivetés.

It may be possible to encounter and respect mystery
without art and music and story and ritual.
However, too many seem to think
that one can and should,
although our heritage has always believed
the exact opposite,
from the New Testament hymns on.

(Gleaned from an article
by and with the approval of
Andrew Greeley)

New Ways

My heart aches with the state of Our Church.

The hierarchy would suffocate us with control.

Rigidity prevents it finding
contemporary solutions to contemporary challenges.

The institutional dread of deviating from orthodoxy
inhibits, indeed, prohibits us
from using the Holy Spirit's Gifts
of Imagination and Creativity.

The bureaucratic suppression of Our Church
will be laid to rest in the pages of history,
a mere chapter
that leads to another unfolding of the Christian Story.

I'm driven to help hasten its demise
but also prepare for the inevitable:

The Birth of New Ways to be Church.

Message from a Friend

Many Catholics like me have just left the room,
<u>for good</u>,
found new homes and avoid all the institutional crap
for what it is,
old style clerics trapped in historical dogmas
and hollow prayers and rituals
providing false answers to questions
no one is asking anymore.

Many of us have gotten past the energy needed
to care about reform, renewal,
or any other radical transformation
of a dead institution.

As I have said before,
when an institution in the 21st century
elects a new leader
and half of it legitimate membership
is formally and solemnly excluded
from authentic participation in that election,
that institution no longer has any historical or
legitimate claim to allegiance of any kind.
It is so blinded by its history and ideology
it cannot see truth before it ---
and the sin against it is perpetuating.

So I live in faith as a Catholic,
An ecumenical independent sacramental Catholic,
but no longer Roman in any way.

I claim my heritage as a Catholic
but denounce its current Roman manifestations
as gross trivializations of a great, albeit flawed,
diverse, sacramental, biblical, scientific,
intellectual, service, communitarian,
peace and justice tradition.

But I deny them my allegiance
until they embrace their history
and current demands of the world
for a renewed presence in the authentic spirit
of the Reign of God.

Peace Always,

XXXXXX

Ode to One Seeking a smaller "purer" church

Blessed am I
that your vision of church
is so exclusive
as to accept ONLY
those of your extreme viewpoint.

Blessed are Thee
that My Vision of True Church
is Inclusive enough
to accept even those of
your extreme viewpoint.

Thanks, God.

Openness

Those who adhere
to specific religious doctrines
may feel threatened
by globalization,
by the world becoming localized
at an increasing rate,
by other religious beliefs.

Often, they retreat into fundamentalist enclaves
denying any possibility of
Enrichment through Diversity.

Some, like St. Basil the Great, believe that
the integrity of religious experience
can be preserved by
an appreciation for different faiths,
reflecting a deep understanding of
one's own faith.

Sipping from even the most exotic flowers
Is not a source of corruption,
but indeed, an opening into

The Life of the Spirit

at the source of

all True Religion.

Path to an Accountable Church

We must first
recognize and name our oppression.
This beginning of the movement
from being victims of history
as defined by someone else
to becoming subject of our own history
is called Conscientization.

We must reclaim our adulthood
from those who have reinforced
infantilization of the Laity.

We must achieve
A Voice in the Church,
to be taken seriously
on a par with other voices,
clerical, priestly, Episcopal.

We must voice our vast reservoir of Practical Wisdom
Theologically and Ethically.

We must cast aside
attempts by hierarchy to stifle debate.

Let us take the emphasis off Church as Institution
and Live it more as Community,
People of God,
Inclusive rather than Exclusive,

locating the Heart of Church
in the Life of the Community,
not in organization.

A Priesthood

For nearly a thousand years
Our priests were not socially distinct
from us.

There no seminaries;
One simply presented himself
three days before Ordination
for an oral exam.
If over 24 years old
with no physical defects,
and a grasp of the Faith
and communication skills,
one was ordained a priest.

Our priest was hardly distinguishable
From us.

Oh yes,
Our priests were more literate than most of us,
but they had to work the fields
just as we.

Then in the middle ages,
the pontiffs
revamped priesthood
into a disciplined army
marching in-step with the Pope,
set off from our "profane" occupations,
with special uniforms,
bent on ruling us,
a subservient laity.

We were then excluded from all participation
With Mass becoming
the priest's business,
with us as spectators.

Altar garb set him apart,
and he whispered prayers
in a language we understood not.

We were separated from it
by a thick railing,
no longer allowed to bring up
ordinary bread for consecration.

No longer could we receive the bread in our hands
standing up;
We were forced to kneel and receive it
on our tongues.

The Chalice was withheld.

And forced celibacy further set us apart.

And when the Protestants
embraced the Universal Priesthood,

The Catholic Church reacted with reactive zeal
to further differentiate "our" priests
and all they did
was Sanctified even more.

The very foundations of Christianity
were said to rest on
a Sacred Priesthood.

And then Vatican II

And then the sex abuse scandal

A discovery:

A view of the priest as Sacred
obscures or replaces
his status
as one of the baptized,
as another sinner, like us, needing redemption.

A view of the priest as sacred obscures
his humanity.

We have made Baptism nothing
And
Ordination everything.

Church life is ultimately relational;
A relationship between human laity
and
human priests
needs rebuilding.

Parishes need to be run
by priests and laity
In collaboration.

Church official
needs to stop painting
an iconic image or our priests.

Instead,
The new Vatican Instruction
which delineates the role of parish priests
tells us the priest
is in charge
by dint of his ordination
and "father" to us all.

The "cultic" model of priest
Espoused by the Vatican
will be a tragedy for church.

Icons are beautiful
But brittle and fragile
and shatter with destructive results
(as we have seen).

A Priesthood of all believers
is the true call of Jesus.

Cultic priests are dominant at the moment;
But changing that forever
will be
A coming Priesthood of
Married Men and Women,
Us.

Priestly Grief

So much of Church teaching
Fails to reach people where they are,

And most priests agree with their parishioners.

Priests are called upon to be
A Focus of Unity
In A Church

When deep mutual suspicion
creates extreme polarization.

The Laity
Overwhelmingly blame the Bishops
for the sexual abuse crisis

while priests bear the brunt of the penalty
with little or no support
from on high.

Priestly Grief

Our priests, Like us,
Grieve

The passages of life,
The loss of youth,
The passing of the middle years,
The loss of health,

They Grieve

The loss of Integrity
occasioned by fear or cowardice
The wife and family
Sacrificed to mandatory celibacy
The loss of trust and confidence
following the abuse scandals
The failed leadership of their bishops
The Church's inability to listen
to the anguished voices of women
The loss of morale
occurring with their bishops'
unwillingness
to listen to them

Overwork

Being misunderstood.

The teachings of the Second Vatican Council are being reversed.

Clear evidence of this is found in the fact that discussion is no longer encouraged on such matters as sexuality, contraception, homosexuality, women's ordination and celibacy

in favor of the definitive pre-Vatican II positions.

The issue of clergy sexual abuse
and the cover-up by bishops
is re-establishing a closed, secret,
and unaccountable mode of operating
in the Church as it was 50 years ago.

The response to the current priest shortage

is to hearken back to the era before Vatican II

in an attempt to re-create

the same spiritual

and social environment

that fostered so many vocations.

The emergence of women's issues in the Church correlates with the decline in religious vocations

which in turn has contributed greatly to current crisis in Catholic education.

As a result a returned to cloistered

and veiled nuns is sought.

Above all, the issue of Church authority is key.

An educated, and now outraged, laity is
questioning the secrecy and unaccountability

in way the Church operates

and even the authority of the Church itself.

The absolute authority of Popes, bishops, and priests

is being challenged by knowledgeable decisions of
an informed conscience.
But there is hope.

True hope is not a longing for something

that is not known.

True hope must always be a longing

for what we know should be.

Dissent has been in the Church from the beginning.

Look no further than the very first days

of the early Church

as described in the Gospels, the Acts of the Apostles
and the letters of Paul and John

to fully appreciate the tensions that have been, and always will be,

alive and well in the Church.

There is a life-giving spirit in the tensions

that generally accompanies love for one another.

While it is good to hope for what we know should be,

it is well to remember

that its fullness will never be achieved here.

Righting the wrongs of centuries.

Official Church is guilty of misogyny,
in its theology, in its interpretation of scripture,
in its exclusion of women from any significant position
in Church governance,
even in its history,
which has scanted women's contributions to the
Church in every sphere.

The new pope has a duty
to encourage the preservation of female memory
and tradition,
and the uprooting of a false tradition
which has made women
the sources of sin and temptation
and the dwelling place of evil.

John Paul II reversed many of the strides
made after Vatican II
toward equality of women in the Church.
A good many women
have completed degrees in pastoral ministry,
but, in the latter years of John Paul's reign,
found themselves shut out of priest-less parishes
that sorely needed them.

Why do we have
thousands of unemployed lay ministers
- most of them women –
unless it is more preferable to close parishes
than to allow women to maintain the very lifeblood
of a communal Church?

The pope
has to address the women's question.
It is a major issue of our time.

Recognizing it can only strengthen this papacy
and this Church.

The papacy, and church-official,
can only be diminished by ignoring it.

Silent Oppression

Catholic Tradition squanders Lay Experience.

Laypeople have neither active, nor passive voice.

Laypeople are not elected to office in the Church,
nor do we vote.

Understandable
when Clergy were educated,
Lay Not.
Hardly so, today.

Why no organized attempt to change this?
The systemic
and structural
Oppression of the Laity

The division between clergy and laity
in Catholic Tradition
systematically subordinates and undervalues
Lay
lifestyle, talent, leadership, experience, and
Spirituality.

Though the hierarchy would never admit it publicly,
their patterns of behavior
and the structures within the Catholic Church
treat the Laity
as if they have lesser talent and
are of lesser account.

Enough!

Spirituality/Sexuality

Human Sexuality
once was perceived as
A component of the Spiritual,
A Central aspect of it.

Everything in existence
Springs forth from the Cosmic Womb of
Unlimited Possibility.

The Spiritual and Sexual capacity of humans
Flows from the Spiritual Energy of
Creation
Opening Faith.

Sexuality
is about a deep capacity for
Love.

Religions have dishonored
Sexuality, Spirituality, Creativity,
by maintaining that
God has nothing to do with Sexuality.

Religions urge us to
Transcend Eros and passion
rather than to
Integrate them into our Living.

Religious Creeds
Demonize
Goddess
A Central Figure of our Ancient Ancestors
because of her
Incredible capacity for
Sexuality and Creativity.

We need to rediscover
what Sexuality is all about.
When we honor
The Sacred Mystery of Sexuality,
We embrace the deepest human mystery
and
God's Divine Mystery.

Sexuality
is about
Creativity.

Spirituality
Honors the Whole Person.

Religion tends to offer
only otherworldly utopias,
ideals of unreachable perfection.

We need
Connection
Here and Now.

The primary sin
is not disobedience,
But Disconnection.

Surprise

I have been trying
to figure out
by whose authority
the hierarchy in place
sets all these rules

to Exclude people.

Jesus
defied the hierarchy in-place
at his time
with His rampant

Inclusiveness.

Alas,
I have found the culprits;
It is us.

Not only do we empower
the abusers,
we pay for it.

Enough!

Though the guidance is all around me,

the answers are deep within me.

Though I can see God in everything and everyone
I meet,
I connect with the Divine within me too.

Though I seek answers to the questions of Life,
I am learning simply to Live the Questions.

Though I suffer Life's losses,
I grow with the Divine Love
which sees me
through them.

The Labyrinth of Life
Simply brings me back to where I am,
Renewed
for having Connected with

The Truth at My Center.

Trust in Whom

We trust that sooner or later,
Sancta Sophia will bear witness
to the truth in our Church,
and is using us as instruments to do so in the process.
Meanwhile, is it possible
the Holy Spirit God is inspiring the Pope and bishops
to behave in ways that expose
the moral bankruptcy of an authoritarian structure
in which the "appearance" of virtue is valued
more than transparency and accountability?
Is Sancta Sophia exposing the "image" of holiness
in contrast to the true and genuine article?

A good image is a projection of goodness.
We trust our impressions or images gained from
experience or from others to guide us.
We can know goodness and truth.

To err is human
but when the hierarchy expands the error
it is a major league betrayal of trust.
The problem is not only the revealed wrong-doing,
but more importantly the obfuscation
and disremembering,
perceived as lies,
that they use to protect an image
different from reality.
This is called hypocrisy,
and is the one sin that Jesus really got upset about.
Secrecy, lack of accountability,
and obstruction of justice
should upset us as well.

When the purpose of declaring bankruptcy
is to hide incriminating evidence,
image is more important than reality.

(Gleaned from the ARCC
Association for the Rights of Catholics in the Church)

Two kinds of Celibacy in the Priesthood

Charismatic Celibacy
(A Gift Given)
is
Liberating,
Authoritative,
and
Joyful.

It is packed with Power.

It is
Attractive,
Fascinating,
and
Real.

Charismatic Celibacy is Sacramental.

Mandatory Celibacy
(forced)

dis-empowers,
drains psychic energy,
distracts
and
detracts.

It is
Lonely,
drives
alternate compensations
and is often
destructive
and
lethal.

Charismatic Celibacy cannot be mandated.

(A message from Donald Cozzen's book
"Freeing Celibacy.")

We Want it Back!

Jesus Christ started it all
by calling us to priesthood.

We lived our faith
And worshipped together
sometimes in hiding,
often in our homes.

We celebrated Eucharist together
In many ways
In many places.

Somewhere along the way
We abandoned church
to a group of celibate male clerics,
to a hierarchy of power.

As is typical with hierarchical organizations,
the mission was lost
for the sake of perpetuating the organization
and the jobs within.

We ended up worshipping
only where and how the hierarchy told us we could,
or for most,
not at all.

The people to whom we entrusted church
have screwed it up.

And now we want it back!

The Holy Spirit
--clearly on our side—
is helping us retrieve our church
by helping us take it over at the grass roots
and
by concluding the all-male all-celibate ordained
priesthood.

We want our Church back
And
We'll get it!

When we uncover our veiled selves,

revealing the mirrors we are,
the Light of God
grows brighter and brighter
and we are turned into
the Divine Image we reflect.

This is the work of the Holy Spirit.

Paraphrased from 2 Corinthians 3:18

Where is God

I searched for God
in my complicated, confused,
sometimes chaotic life.

Sure, I found God
in Church, in Sacrament, and in many Sacred Places
and Events.
But I also discovered God
in the ordinary experiences of my life,
where Faith and Life seem to merge.

I found out that
all ground is Holy Ground.

For too much of my life,
I failed to see the preciousness of
each ordinary human experience.

I swam through life,
not fully sensing that
God is near me, with me, in me,
and beyond me.

I could not exist
without God's sustaining Love.

God is a heartbeat away.

God's in the kitchen as well as the chapel,

if I have eyes to see.

Whither the Institution?

The divine right model of authoritarian hierarchical Church

adopted from the Roman Empire and solidified during the middle ages

is fundamentally and aggressively resisting adaptation to evolutionary change

accelerating its rush towards historical irrelevancy and to extinction.

How do I love Church?

I Love Church with the Loving imperative that it change and Grow.

I have learned that

simply resting in the belief that the Holy Spirit will sustain the Church

is really a cop-out.

It is a denial of the radical institutionalism

which has for centuries placed

Hierarchy before Member,

Power before Love,

Authority of Exclusion over Inclusion,

Male Domination over Truth and Justice,

Hammer over Heart.

All attempts of reform at the edges

have proven to be non-viable.

So too is the retreat into the delusion

of a fundamentalist resistance to contemporary
reality,

a current naïve option of some.

The institution which made possible,

protected and sustained

systemic and systematic abuse of children

while defrauding us of our donations,

cannot be trusted to correct itself;

it defies reason and credibility to think it could do so

while maintaining the characteristics

which made it possible in the first place.

This is likely only one of the many abuses

to which any unaccountable, divine right,
totalitarian organization

is inevitably susceptible.

Retreat, yes.

but not to the retreat of the foolhardy,

convinced that running away

is in fact regrouping for the attack,

rather, a retreat into Inclusive Reflection

and Prayerful

Quest for the Message and Mission, the Core,

the Christ

devoid of self- or institutional self-interest.

Jesus and His message must be saved from the
slavery of the hierarchy

just as the chosen people were freed

from the slavery of the ancient Egyptians.

The hierarchy offers us a "Jesus",

in the Blessed Sacrament

ensconced in a chalice with a cover, under a cloth,

in the tabernacle,

locked within a building over which the
impenetrable institution of hierarchy

holds unaccountable control

(after having been built by the people).

We, the faithful are forced to "come to Jesus"

under the physical and spiritual conditions and
constraints of "Hierarchy",

designed historically as a control mechanism over
the unruly and unholy.

Institutionally, Jesus does not seem to be True Love,

but rather a captive within a castle,

cut off from his people and from the pursuit of His
mission of salvation.

Successive layers of

clergy, monsignors, bishops, archbishops, cardinals,
and popes

have convinced themselves that they alone are

the keepers of the message.

"Trust us", they demand, not just to God's children

but to God.

Is there an alternative?

The Vineyard

Why does the vineyard produce bad grapes?
Because the caretakers did not do their job!
Instead of producing "righteousness" and "justice"
the vineyard has produced "bloodshed"
and "outcry."

The vineyard is supposed to bear the fruit
of God's reign
that is to be evidenced in the manifestation
of God's character
and action in the world -which being slow to anger,
rich in mercy,
abounding in kindness,
and the action that follows in reaching out
to the poor, the blind, the lame, the leper, the sinner,
the prostitute.

The policies and programs of the vineyard caretakers
is supposed to produce good for others
and to bear evidence of God's mercy, kindness
and justice.

What the programs and policies of the caretakers
produce, however,
is more violence, hatred, prejudice, exclusion
and oppression.

What we see
in the actions of the caretakers of the vineyard,
the bishops of our church,
is the promotion of programs and policies
that produce
hatred, division, exclusion, oppression and more
prejudice.

Whether the people be homosexuals in the church,
or divorced and remarried,
or men who do desire to be married and priests,
and all those who oppose
non-doctrinal positions of the church,
they become victims of the fear, homophobia,
institutional interests
and self-protectionism of the leaders.

What does God say in Isaiah?
And what does Jesus say in Matthew?
What they have will be taken away from them
and given to those who truly practice righteousness
and justice.

Who have truly experienced the grace and the
mercy of God
and who now direct their lives in the freedom
of that encounter with God.
Those who continue to construct walls
of fear, hatred, prejudice and division/exclusion
are not motivated by mercy, forgiveness or love.
And so what they have, their power and their
authority, will be taken from them.

The Levitical, or priestly tradition,
is interested in protecting the power
and authority of the temple
and the power and authority that is rooted
in the absolute obedience of the law.
For the Levitical tradition, laws are ends in
themselves.

The Prophetic tradition
says that the commands of God are the vehicles
that are intended to carry mercy, forgiveness and
love
to the poor, the outcast and the marginal.

The Prophets frequently say that the rituals and rules
are not ends in themselves,
rather the concern of Torah is with feeding the
hungry, visiting the sick, clothing the naked, lifting up
the lowly, reaching out to the needy.

I suspect that if we looked at the ministry of Jesus
we would see that he followed the Prophetic
tradition more than the Levitical tradition.
Frequently he violates the Sabbath laws,
and the religious law of purity
in favor of eating with sinners,
reaching out to the excluded ones.

The problem is that later Christian tradition
redid the story of Jesus
through the levitical tradition (Letter to the Hebrews)
and made the emphasis the blood sacrifice
of Jesus on the cross
rather than the full gift of self in love for others.

Churches/institutions who have a lot invested
in maintaining the Levitical power
have little interest in the prophetic concerns
of the Gospel.

We ask if the programs and policies of the Church
are vehicles of Prophetic power?
or Levitical power?

And are we to be disciples of the priestly tradition
and therefore instruments of prejudice and exclusion
(purity and exclusivity)?
Or are we disciples of the prophetic Jesus
who was willing give his life not for the institution,
but for the poor, the blind, the sinner, the excluded?

Where do we stand
in relation to church institutions
that produce "bloodshed" and "oppression?"

Are we to be instruments of righteousness and
justice?

Or instruments of continued hatred and violence?

Why can't I be a good Catholic and dissent?

Apparently, being a dissenter and a good Catholic

are mutually exclusive.

Why can't I be both?

There is no "Thou shall not dissent" commandment.

Yet today it appears that anyone

who does not strictly follow or agree with the rules
promulgated by Rome

is considered to be a bad Catholic.

And this to the point that Pope

is apparently saying

good riddance—who needs them anyway—

let them fall by the wayside:

they are just weeds in the field.

Why is questioning and asking about change

deemed equal to heresy?

It is akin to being against the war in Iraq and being
labeled anti-American.

This country was formed by a group of dissenters

who believed strongly in freedom of speech

and religion.

Unquestioned, blind followership

has had many a bad result historically—

the Crusades and Hitler to name a few examples.

Jesus Christ Himself was a dissenter.

He objected to the behavior of those

who observed the minutiae of the law,

while ignoring its spirit.

Saint Paul too was a dissenter amongst the apostles.

Saint Paul made a strong distinction

between the letter and the spirit of the law.

Were Christ and Paul labeled as insurgents?
Absolutely—and ultimately they were put to death

for their beliefs.

Much has been written about the various crises

within the Roman Catholic Church,

including declining church attendance

in Europe and North America,

declining numbers of religious clergy

and practices of the so-called "Cafeteria Catholics."

An archbishop closed one seminary

and reopened a more conservative one

where no dissension is tolerated.

There appears to be no solution

offered for the clergy crisis, except to

"pray for vocations"

and institute a national prayer day for vocations.

Forced by the paucity of priests,

the church has opened its doors to allow and
encourage deacons (who may be married),

yet they too can only do so much.

Much sacramental activity is still

the sole purview of the priests.

Requests to allow priests to marry

or allow women to become priests

have fallen on deaf ears in Rome.

There are no valid reasons for preventing either

marriage in the priesthood or

women in the priesthood.

An objection to married priesthood is that having a
family or spouse would dilute the priest's devotion

to serving God and the people,

while celibacy allows undivided devotion.

How insulting to the apostles

and ministers of other religious traditions

to make such pious statements.

As for women in the priesthood, an objection is that
all the apostles were men.

Who was more inclusive than Christ?

He spoke with women from other religions,

ate with women, and

had women in His entourage.

After He rose from the dead,

He first appeared to Mary of Magdala.

Coincidence?

I think not.

This issue is about power.

As for dissenters,

they are not welcome because they threaten

the order.

They make those in power pause and reconsider,
which is always uncomfortable,

as was shown by

the firing of the editor of *America* magazine.

The church has always had its pendulum swings, like
everything else in life.

The pendulum now is so far to the right

that the church will apparently brook

no dissent by anyone

and is trying to exclude anyone

who does not keep in lockstep with its teachings.

History has taught us what happens

when decrees are issued

and people blindly follow them.

Despite Rome's expressed support

for the separation of church and state,

it was a huge contributor

to the reelection of the President by its decree,

issued through its bishops,

whereby they proclaimed

those who voted for other candidates

could be denied Communion.

The Catholic Church today may not want dissenters,

but it has them.

Being a dissenter should not, *ipso facto*,

equal being a bad Catholic.

Asking for change

when it is necessary, valuable, and appropriate

is different,

yet Rome does not appear to see the difference.

Hope in the face of discouragement

What troubles people is some of the discouragement
that they find in the church.

"Why should I continue to be a Catholic?

Why belong to the church?"

They're looking for leadership and they're not finding
it or

they're finding a kind of leadership that seems

to be pushing them away.

There are a couple of things that happened

that many people found very discouraging:

married people being told,

"If you practice birth control, don't come to
Communion,"

almost as though we had never written in 1968

a pastoral letter called

Human Life in our Day

which made it clear

that this was a matter for individual conscience,

made it clear that there is a right, and a responsibility

even, to dissent within the church.

Now all that seems to be forgotten.

People are pushed away and told don't come.

A few years ago a Bishops' letter welcomed

gay and lesbian people into our community.

Now they seem to say,

"No, we say we want you, but, in fact,

unless you change what they now call an
'inclination,'

you're not very welcome."

We also find our church leadership failing

to speak out

on this violent war that is going on.

And, throughout our country, we feel

a lack of leadership

as we find our churches being closed.

And we hear our church leaders say,

"Well, we have to follow the demographics.

Our Catholic people are moving out;

therefore, we go with them."

Forgetting that the cities are the most

poverty-stricken,

where the church ought to be present

more vibrantly than ever.

Of course it is a very racist thing, too,

because where we are closing our churches

is 83 percent African American

so we're walking away saying,

"We don't really need you or

need to be among you."

So people are discouraged

because of what is happening,

but if we listen very deeply to the Scriptures today

we can find reason to develop within our hearts

a sense of hopefulness.

We need to put ourselves into the time of Jeremiah

when they had been promised by God

that they would have leadership

starting with King David, who was the ideal king,

and then they would have that kind of leadership.

Now suddenly they don't.

They find that one of their kings, Ahaz, is an apostate.

Another is Zedekiah who is totally weak

and incompetent, unable to lead the people.

Jeremiah proclaims how the people need to be faithful

to God and to the covenant,

but they're not, so they're overwhelmed

by the Babylonian army and carried off into exile.

And yet, in the midst of all that, Jeremiah is able to say, speaking for God,

"The days are coming when I shall fulfill the gracious promise that I made

in favor of Israel and Judah.

In those days and at that time

I will make him who is the shoot of righteousness

sprout from David's line.

He will practice justice and righteousness in the land.

He will be called, Yahweh, our Justice, our Holiness."

That's a powerful image that Jeremiah is using
because he could see what was happening.
The leadership was deteriorating,
and so they could picture it as,
instead of a full, blossoming tree,
just a stump. That's all that was left.
It seemed to be dead.
And yet there was to be a shoot
that would come from that stump
and give new life, break into new fullness.
The shoot that was to come, this new life,
Jeremiah is looking forward to the time of Jesus.
Jesus will come.
The very Son of God will be that new shoot.
God our righteousness,
God our holiness,
God our justice is Jesus.
Jeremiah, Isaiah, the other prophets,
could look forward to that and so they had hope.
And, of course, we're looking forward now,

to remember once more that moment

when Jesus came into the world –

where he brought the message of God's love,

where he brought his way, his truth and his light

for us to follow.

So how can we not be hopeful

if we commit ourselves to Jesus?

The Gospel lesson makes it so clear.

Jesus is talking about, first of all,

the destruction of the temple that took place

in 71 A.D.

when the Roman armies invaded the Holy Land.

Then he also projects that to the end of time.

But the end is also a beginning.

One thing ends, but then new life comes.

As the world in our time in history, moves on,
disappears,

the Reign of God can break forth in its fullness.

Jesus has come and proclaimed that

the Reign of God is near.

And then as God continues to be with us in Jesus,

Emmanuel -- God with us, that Reign of God

can come into its fullness.

And the Word of God, of course, is trustworthy.

Jeremiah knew that, Isaiah knew that

and so they knew that out of that stump of Jesse

would come new life.

That's what Jesus tells us. "Yes, there is an ending,

but there is a new beginning –

we can have hope in that.

The Reign of God is present in our midst,"

Jesus tells us.

St. Paul instructs us what to do

while that Reign of God is in our midst

waiting to be brought to its fullness.

"Love one another. Do good to one another,"

"For the rest, brothers and sisters,

we ask you in the name of Jesus,

we urge you to live in a way that pleases God.

This you do, but try to do more.

You know the instructions we gave you

on behalf of Jesus.

The will of God for you is to become holy.

Let each of you love one another."

So while we're waiting for the Reign of God to come

in its fullness,

we prepare for it by deepening our spirit

of love for one another.

We can make that Reign of God happen

in that part of the world in which we live,

where we are, where we spend every day,

by following what Jesus tells us,

what Jesus showed us,

by bringing love and goodness and kindness

wherever we go.

This is the way that we will really celebrate.

Yes, we can be discouraged,

but we can also have hope,

trusting in God's Word.

Jesus has come.

He will come again.

In the meantime he is with us

as we make the Reign of God come into its fullness.

This can be a time of great joy
and also a time of great hope
as we continue to listen deeply to God's Word
and to try to follow more faithfully the way of Jesus
and we'll discover a deep sense of joy and hope
in our hearts.

(From a homily by Bishop Tom Gumbleton)

Sexuality

Sexuality is

A Beautiful,
Good,
Extremely Powerful,
Sacred Energy,
Given us by God,
and
Experienced in every cell of Our Being,
as
An Irrepressible Urge
To Overcome Our Incompleteness,
To Move Towards Unity,
and
Consummation
with that which is beyond us.

It is the Pulse
To Celebrate,
To Give and Receive Delight,
To Find Our Way Back
To Paradise
where
We Can be Naked,
Shameless, and
Without Worry
as
We Make Love in the Moonlight.

Chasing Silence

When I spoke,
or even wrote,
or even thought of Silence,
I lost it.

It was as if this strange being,
beyond description,
was missing from life.

Monasteries can trap Silence
in a cage,
making it
a mere restriction on speech,
but this strange creature
only seems to approach
on its own
as if intimidated by a leash.

I found that
although the absence of noise
is friends with Silence,
when my head was full
of echoes of myself,
Silence never even brushed my ankle.

I struggled to still my mind.
But often the battle of doing that
became a huge project,
another noise.

A Master said,
"Do-not other than not-doing."

All I had to do
is
Not do.

Why is the simplest approach
the most difficult?

I'll take on a challenge,
but this seems too simple,
albeit far from easy.

No process I know
coaxes it from hiding.

I must become
an empty field.

Accepting my own darkness
might bring on the Light.

Accepting my own heaviness
might bring a Lightness.

This creature Silence
seems to need
emptiness in me
to move near.

I guess
the less said,
or written,
or even thought
about Silence,
the better.

(S l l e n c e)

Silence speaks for itself;
all my efforts to seek it
chase it away
and
smack of perjury.

Creation

Creation is an expression of God's Love.

It's distinction is its Gratuity.
It is a Free Gift of Love with no strings attached.
Else it would be imperfect.

God gives the world to itself,
as the place where humans live out our destiny
to be
human.

Made in the image and likeness of God,
we have the potential
to Love as God Loves
in the real world.

We have to make the world
a more truly human reality,
failing through fear or greed,
succeeding through courage and generosity.

The Sacred
is not something God imposes
on top of secular history,
or
Grace producing a supernatural dimension
of the human person
grafted upon a secular original.

There is one history;
The Church is a worldly reality.

Our Desire for God
is not grafted on to our secular base,
but is a Natural Expression
of Humans as created by God.

The secular
is not some godless reality
requiring some special Divine Act
to open it to the Holy.

The secular is already Graced.
Nature is Graced.
The world is already Sacred
(whether or not we know it.)
Grace is everywhere.

The world and human beings
are already open to the infinite,
especially when they follow the natural order.

The humanization of the world,
by whomever,
is the world growing into
God's Plan.

Our struggle toward
A Fuller Humanity
is
Salvation History.

We are secular beings.
We live and breathe in the world.
The world lives and breathes in us.
We are people in a human world.

We are organisms in a material universe.
We live simultaneously
in a world of meanings
and
causes and effects.

The struggle for meaning
and
The Experience of Chaos
are inescapably
part of the secular reality.

Any religion that suggests
the world is not our home
misreads Incarnational Theology.

We are born, live, and die
within the secular world.
Being religious
cannot be something that relativizes
the secularity
that is part of our very being.

Freedom

Jesus gifted us with Freedom.

As He stated in His Sermon on the Mount,
Through Love,
We can be free from
Worldly securities,
The Need for constant pleasure,
Power, control and approval,
Conventional wisdom,
Over-identification with a group,
Our hurts,
Lack of forgiveness,
Our minds,
Results,
and Self possessiveness.

Yet, Institutions
even Church
try and take away
these Christ-given gifts.

They encourage us to

Find Security outside ourselves, in them,
Relinquish power and control to them,
Rely on their wisdom,
Identify totally with them,
Seek forgiveness through them,
Keep it mental,
but not think for ourselves.

Who gave these institutions the right
to take away
Our Gift of Freedom?

What made us so weak-kneed
to relinquish
Our Gift of Freedom?

From Wisdom

God,
To You,
The Whole Universe is like a grain of sand
Or a drop of morning dew.

You love all of creation
And loathe nothing that You have made,
Else it would not exist.

For nothing could exist
Unless You will it;
Nothing could be
Unless sustained by You.

All that exists is Yours,
Oh Lover of Souls,
For Your Eternal Spirit is in all things.

You teach us little by little,
As we are able to learn from our mistakes
And grow in Love
In You,
Oh God.

Gratitude

The fact that my roof leaked
allows me to
Appreciate a dry house when it rains.

The fact that my sewer backed up
allows me to
Appreciate each and every flush.

The fact that my youth was spent in a city apartment
allows me to
Appreciate my house
and
Torch Lake.

The fact that my blood pressure was high
allows me to
Appreciate the Un-Stress of Letting Go.

The fact that my son nearly died several times
allows me to
Appreciate Him
And
Mayo Clinic doctors.

The fact that he finally died
Allows me to
Appreciate Him
and
Hospice.

The fact that I worked hard for Ford for 32 years
allows me to
Appreciate my Life hereafter (Ford.)

That fact that I spent so much of my life
focused on me
allows me to
Appreciate Loving Others
and
being Loved.

Without the down sides,
I guess
I'd never fully appreciate
All my wonderful gifts.

Thanks, God.

Everything Belongs.

Awareness

I have come to believe
That when Anthony DeMello defined Spirituality
as
Awareness,
and further as
Awareness, Awareness, Awareness,
He did not mean
simple conscious receiving.

I believe he did not mean
receiving, accumulating, interpreting,
storing up, judging, compiling, and modifying.
That would seem
so unlike Anthony DeMello.

Even looking with more than eyes
to weigh, balance, and receive
would not seem to fit his definition.

I believe he may have meant
An Awareness
that looks, sees, listens
without consciousness;
An Awareness
in which there is no receiving,
a total movement of freedom.

An Awareness
which has no center from which it moves,
thus able to move in all directions
without the barrier of time and space.
It is looking which is total
a listening which is total
an awareness which is total.
His Awareness,
I believe,
is the essence of Attention,
the kind of Attention Mother Theresa gave
to the one present with her in any moment,
an Attention without distraction,
without thought.

Thought is never still,
reaction expressing itself in thought
further increasing responses.
Love and Beauty
cannot be contained in thought.
There are no opposites
to Love and Beauty,
while there are opposite thoughts.

Anthony DeMello's Awareness,
I believe,
is seeing without thought,
without word,
without the response from memory,
totally different than
seeing with thought and memory.
Those are superficial and partial,
not really seeing at all.

His Awareness,
I believe,
Is seeing without thought,
total seeing.

To have any chance of attaining it,
I must be perfectly still and Aware
to gain a glimpse of the totality of life.

Join me in the Precious Present Moment
of Candle Light

The candle
creates pools of light
and
ever-changing shadows
at the edge of the pool
where I am aware of other things
but not distracted by them.

The intensity of the candle light
is thus enhanced
and that which is lit by it
emphasized.

Sometimes, it burns strong and steady,
without movement or hesitancy,
holding its shape,
strong, round the short blackened wick.

At other times,
the flame bounces and jumps round its seat,
caught by a draft,
dancing and vibrant,
now one way, now the other.

The candle flame,
intense, moving, wavering, aspiring,
is a longing to be with God,
and
a glimpse of the Light and Fire
that is God.

the very nature of candle light
is self-consuming.
Burning a wick set in a candle
is time-limited.
Fueled by the wax,
and so diminishing with each passing hour,
the candle remains alight
until there is no longer enough wax
to sustain the wick.
It then collapses
and extinguishes itself.
The flame is gone.

The wax of the candle
changes from solid to liquid
as the heart of the flame causes the wax to melt
and feed the wick
until gradually the reservoir of liquid wax
broadens and deepens.

the candle left in a draft burns erratically,
the flame drawn over to one side,
unevenly melting the wax core
until the wall of wax gives way
and the wax pool begins to leak down
the side of the candle.
At that point,
the wick burns long
and begins to smoke
is no longer a safe light,
becoming unpredictable
and needing to be extinguished.

The candle flame
is a Light of Silence
no buzz or hum,
just a lit silence
and a changing pattern between shadow and light.

Low in the body of the candle,
the glow from the energy
lightens the candle wall
until the whole candle seems alit.
Inside, the wax glistens brightly
and gently drips from the wall to the pool.

Gradually, it consumes itself
and the lit silence
drifts into the night. A candle blown or snuffed out,
loses its light suddenly
and the blackened wick gives off a swirl of blue
smoke,
twisting and curling upwards
beyond the spent candle
until it suddenly becomes detached from its source
and its movement lost
leaving behind
a slight drifting haze and
distant smell of wax.

Who is Helping

I often feel so inadequate

attempting to be of some help to others

experiencing terrible losses

and

Grief.

But then,

I simply remind myself,

that I *Am* inadequate

in the face of such suffering,

but that *it is not I*

that provides any healing grace;

It is the Divine

and I must simply try and be

an instrument

of God's Peace.

Grace

I never started out, nor ever dreamt,
to be a spiritual guide
or emotional companion
for those on life's Grief Journey.

It has been pure Grace.

It came about because I was given
the immense privilege and gift
of being taken
inside the lives of the countless people
I have met
in my Grief and Spiritual Growth Ministries.

What brought us into kinship
was the discovered God-given ability
to travel inward,
to connect the inner experience
with the outer experience,
and to trust that
the Divine is found
in all of Life's experiences.

The willingness to be *open to Growth*,
to keep *climbing the Mountain of Life*,
to give self over to
Transformation
by continual *Attentiveness* to
the movement of the *Holy Spirit* in our lives
has changed many of my fellow travelers
and in the process,
me.

Truly Free

I just realized,
I'm going to die soon.

Oh, relax; maybe not tomorrow,
or even next week,
but soon;
certainly in relation to the 70 years
with which I've been blessed so far.

I just truly realized it;
maybe for the first time.
And you know what?

It's totally freeing.

What is it that I need to fret or worry about?
What's so important that I need to get all upset?
Whom do I need to impress?

I'm going to die soon;
can't do anything about that,
so why not just plain enjoy the day?

Acceptance of my death is totally freeing.
(Wish I'd realized this sooner.)

Though the guidance is all around me,

the answers are deep within me.

Though I can see God in everything and everyone I meet,
I connect with the Divine within me too.

Though I seek answers to the questions of Life,
I am learning simply to Live the Questions.

Though I suffer Life's losses,
I grow with the Divine Love which sees me
Through them.

The Labyrinth of Life
Simply brings me back to where I am,
Renewed
for having Connected with

The Truth at My Center.

Association for the Rights of Catholics in the Church

ARCC's MISSION

is to bring about substantive structural change

in the Catholic Church,

and to institutionalize a collegial understanding

of Church

in which decision-making is shared

and accountability is realized

among Catholics of every kind and condition.

It affirms that there are fundamental rights

which are rooted in the humanity

and baptism of all Catholics.

To this end ARCC developed and works to implement

a Charter of the Rights of Catholics in the Church

and a Proposed Catholic Constitution.

These documents and others

can be found at http://arccsites.org

All are welcomed to join in this effort by joining ARCC.

Made in the USA